LIFE
SCIENCE
STORIES

Adaptation and Survival

Louise and
Richard
Spilsbury

Raintree is an imprint of Capstone Global Library Limited,
a company incorporated in England and Wales having its
registered office at 264 Banbury Road, Oxford OX2 7DY
– Registered company number: 6695582

www.raintree.co.uk
myorders@raintree.co.uk

Produced for Raintree by Calcium
Edited by Sarah Eason and Harriet McGregor
Designed by Paul Myerscough and Geoff Ward
Picture research by Rachel Blount
Production by Victoria Fitzgerald
Originated by Capstone Global Library Limited © 2016
Printed and bound in China

ISBN 978 1 4747 1572 0 (hardback)
19 18 17 16 15
10 9 8 7 6 5 4 3 2 1

ISBN 978 1 4747 1578 2 (paperback)
20 19 18 17 16
10 9 8 7 6 5 4 3 2 1

British Library Cataloguing in Publication Data
A full catalogue record for this book is available
from the British Library.

Acknowledgements
We would like to thank the following for permission
to reproduce photographs: Shutterstock: 312010 23,
Johan Barnard 16, Sylvie Bouchard 20, Davidpstephens
6, Defpicture 14, Maria Dryfhout 24, FloridaStock
22, Joshua Haviv 7, Holbox 12, 13, Jadimages 10,
Javarman 29, Cathy Keifer 18, Peter Kirillov 21, Tamara
Kulikova 15, Marcokenya 17, Rob McKay 11, Pakul54 8,
Przemyslaw 19, Becky Sheridan 28, Audrey Snider-Bell
25, Victor Soares 27, Brendan van Son 5, Jordan Tan 9,
Tramper 4, Mogens Trolle 26.

Cover photographs reproduced with permission of:
Shutterstock: Kjersti Joergense.

Every effort has been made to contact copyright holders
of material reproduced in this book. Any omissions will
be rectified in subsequent printings if notice is given
to the publisher.

> Some words are shown in bold, **like this**. You can
> find out what they mean by looking in the glossary.

Contents

Ways to survive 4

Great white killer 6

Giraffe meals 8

Owl flight 10

Monkey moves 12

Crocodile smile 14

Racing cat 16

Chameleon colour 18

Snow bear 20

Spider's trap 22

Snake attack 24

Zebra journey 26

Changing world 28

Glossary 30

Find out more 31

Index 32

Ways to survive

Animals must change to help them stay alive in their **habitat**. This is called **adaptation**. The change could be to the animal's body or the way in which it behaves. Adaptations can help an animal to hunt or eat, move, find a **mate** or protect itself. Different types of animals have adapted in different ways over thousands of years.

Meet the mole

Moles have adaptations that help them to survive underground. They have sharp claws for digging tunnels in the soil. They also have a large nose to smell earthworms, and sharp teeth to hold on to the worms when they catch them.

Moles have tiny eyes. They do not need to see well because they live in the dark.

This black male frigate bird has **inflated** its bright red throat pouch in order to be noticed!

THE FRIGATE BIRD

Frigate birds are adapted to life in the air. Their 2-metre- (6-feet-) long wings help them swoop down to snatch fish from the sea, and fly off again. They are great flyers but cannot walk or swim well. They only land on cliffs to rest or find a mate. Male frigate birds have another amazing adaptation. They can blow up their red throat pouch like a balloon to attract a female mate!

Great white killer

The great white shark is an incredible hunter. It is one of the most successful **predators** in the oceans. This enormous shark has many **adaptations** for hunting.

Fast and furious

The great white shark has an amazing sense of smell. It can sense a single drop of blood in the water from 5 kilometres (3 miles) away. Its torpedo-like body helps it to swim at speeds of up to 24 kilometres (15 miles) per hour. Its powerful tail can push it upwards so fast that it can knock **prey** out of the water!

Great white sharks have 300 razor-sharp, jagged teeth to grab and tear prey. When teeth wear out, new ones grow in their place.

COLOURED TO KILL

Great white sharks have a grey back and a white belly. This colouring is called countershading. It is a type of **camouflage**, an adaptation that helps the shark to sneak up on prey. The top half of the shark is dark. When prey look down from above, the shark blends in with the dark waters below. The bottom half is light. When prey look up from below, the shark blends in with the sunlit waters above it.

This shark's colouring means that by the time most animals realize the shark is near, it is too late!

Giraffe meals

One of the giraffe's favourite foods are leaves from acacia trees. Acacia trees have hard, sharp thorns that stop most animals from eating them. So why can giraffes eat them?

Amazing tongue

A giraffe's tongue is adapted to get around this thorny problem! It is 46 centimetres (18 inches) long and can reach around the acacia thorns to get to the leaves. The tongue grasps the leaves, then plucks them from the tree. The giraffe's mouth also makes a lot of thick, sticky spit called saliva. This covers any thorns the giraffe might swallow to stop them from hurting its insides.

Giraffes have purple and black tongues. Scientists think that this colour protects their tongues from sunburn when reaching for leaves.

A giraffe's neck is about 2 metres (6 feet) long. It has seven bones in it – the same number found in the neck of a person. However, the giraffe's bones are much bigger – each is 25 centimetres (10 inches) long!

Survival story

FOOD FIGHTS

There are a lot of plant eaters in the grasslands where giraffes live. Giraffes have developed a long neck so they can eat leaves high in the trees, where most other plant eaters cannot reach. This **adaptation** means they do not have to **compete** with many other animals for food. Being tall also protects giraffes. It helps them to see hungry lions up to 30 kilometres (19 miles) away.

Owl flight

The owl is an amazing night-time hunter. It has adapted to fly almost silently through the air. Owls catch small animals on the ground. At night, small animals use sound to hear if a **predator** is nearby. Owls use silent flight to catch their **prey**.

Silent and deadly

The owl is able to fly in silence because of the design of its feathers. Owls have large feathers with jagged edges that soften the sound of the flapping wings. The feathers are also coated in a velvety-smooth cover, which soaks up sound. This lets the owl silently swoop down on its prey.

Owls have very sharp beaks, which they use to rip the flesh off prey. Their incredible eyesight helps them to see prey animals in the dark.

THE SNOWY OWL

Snowy owls are birds of prey that live in cold places such as parts of North America and northern Europe. They have adapted to their home by becoming almost white in colour. This **camouflages** the bird against the snow and allows it to **stalk** prey in the air almost unnoticed.

This snowy owl has excellent eyesight. It can even see tiny animals such mice in the undergrowth.

Monkey moves

Spider monkeys are the acrobats of the rainforest! They swing between trees, eating fruits, nuts, eggs and spiders. Living in the treetops means they do not have to **compete** with many other animals for food and space.

Swinging along

The spider monkey has long arms with hook-like hands and long fingers for swinging through the trees. Its strong tail can twist and grip as tightly as its hands. A rough patch of skin at the end of the tail helps it to grip tightly, too. By swinging from its tail, the monkey keeps its hands free to pick food.

Spider monkeys rest high up in the trees. They also sleep in the trees to stay safely away from **predators** below.

Spider monkeys got their name because they look a bit like spiders when they hang from their tails.

Future story

FOREST IN DANGER

Spider monkeys are in danger. They need large areas of tall forests to survive. They are losing their homes to farming, and many trees are being cut down for wood. Spider monkeys are also hunted by people for food. The monkeys call noisily to each other between the trees, which makes them an easy target.

Crocodile smile

Have you ever heard the saying "Never smile at a crocodile"? When a crocodile shows its teeth, it is not smiling back at you! It is getting ready to bite – and a crocodile's bite can be deadly.

Killer jaws

The crocodile's mouth is adapted to grab and tear its **prey**. The crocodile uses its strong jaws and its 60 deadly teeth to bite prey and drag it underwater to drown it. It then spins its own body to tear off chunks of meat from its victim.

Every one of these teeth is hollow. There is a new tooth growing inside it, ready for use once the old one wears out. A crocodile may go through 3,000 teeth in its lifetime!

SUIT OF ARMOUR

The crocodile has armour-like skin. It is covered in bony scales that overlap like the tiles on a roof. The scales protect the crocodile from scraping its skin on rocks or the ground. They also protect the crocodile from attacks by animals that might otherwise try to eat it.

Crocodiles can **bask** lazily on riverbanks without fear of an attack. Few animals dare to attack an animal protected by sharp teeth and a suit of armour.

Racing cat

The cheetah is the fastest runner in the whole animal world. Its body is adapted to move very quickly over short distances. That is how it catches gazelle and other **prey** that other animals cannot keep up with.

Built for speed

The cheetah has a small head and narrow body. This gives it the perfect shape for speed. Its long legs and bendy backbone help it to take extra-long strides. Its legs are powered by strong muscles and its long tail helps it to balance and steer when making fast turns. The claws on its feet are hard and sharp. They grip the ground better than trainers as the cheetah races along.

Cheetahs can run at 100 kilometres (70 miles) per hour. That is as fast as a car on a motorway.

Can you see the long line of black fur that runs from the cheetah's eye to its mouth? Scientists think this helps to stop glare from the sun during daytime hunting.

Survival story

MASTER OF DISGUISE

A cheetah hunts by day, when prey animals keep a careful lookout for danger. The colour of the cheetah's fur and its spotted **markings** help it to blend in with tall grass. This makes it harder for prey to see it coming.

Chameleon colour

The chameleon can quickly change colour. It can change from green to brown and back faster than you can change your T-shirt! It has adapted in this way to survive in its **habitat**.

Why change colour?

A chameleon changes colour when the light or temperature changes. It also changes colour if its mood changes, such as when it is scared. Most chameleons turn green, yellow, cream or dark brown. A chameleon's normal colour is green or brown. These colours help it to blend in with the trees it lives in. Chameleons **camouflage** themselves to catch their **prey**. They sit hidden among tree leaves and wait for prey to pass by, then shoot out their tongue to catch their meal.

A chameleon's tongue is longer than its body. It shoots out at high speed and traps insect prey on its sticky tip.

SPINNING EYEBALLS

The chameleon's eyes are amazing. Each eye can look in the opposite direction to the other eye. This lets the chameleon look at two things at the same time. If the chameleon sees a **predator** or prey, both eyes look in the same direction to get a clear view.

The chameleon can move its eyes to get a complete view around its whole body.

Snow bear

The polar bear lives in the Arctic at the far north of our planet. This place is covered in ice and snow for most of the year. Incredibly, the polar bear has adapted to survive there.

Fat and fur

The polar bear has two layers of hair. These trap warm air around its body and create a waterproof layer that stops the bear's skin from becoming wet and cold. Polar bear hair looks white but it is see-through. Sunlight passes through the hairs and is soaked up by the bear's black skin. The bear also has a 10-centimetre (4-inch) thick layer of **blubber** all over its body. This acts like a blanket to keep the bear warm.

The polar bear's blubber also helps it to float in the freezing waters of the Arctic.

MELTING ICE

The polar bear travels very long distances to find its **prey**, often drifting on blocks of floating ice. It dives into the water to catch seals from these icy platforms. The polar bear is in danger, though. **Global warming** is melting ice sheets and stopping polar bears from travelling in search of food.

In the future, there may be fewer polar bears. This is because the ice platforms they travel on and hunt from are melting fast.

Spider's trap

All spiders are **predators**. They feed on other small animals, such as insects. Many spiders catch their **prey** by trapping it in their silky webs.

Spinning silk

A spider makes webs from threads of silk. It makes silk inside its body and pushes it out from the end of its **abdomen**. When an insect lands on the web, it becomes stuck or tangled in the silk. As it struggles, the spider feels the web move and rushes out to catch its prey. Some spiders wrap prey in silk before eating it or storing it to eat later.

Spider silk is incredibly strong. It is stronger than a thread of steel of the same thickness!

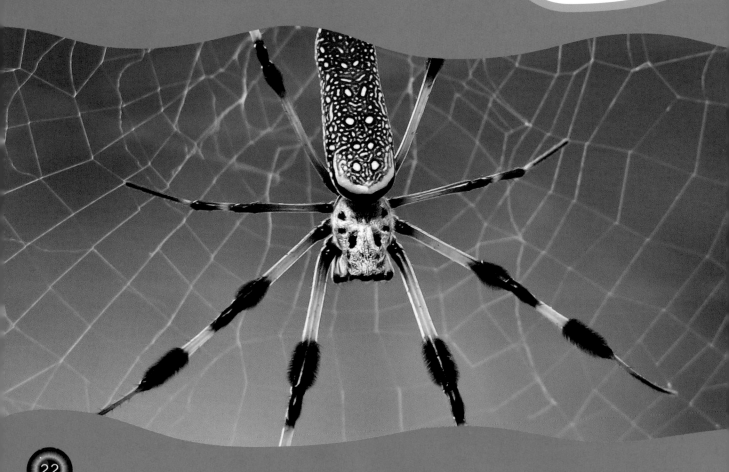

True story

FIRING HAIR DARTS

Many animals try to eat tarantula spiders, including lizards, birds and snakes. Some tarantulas have an **adaptation** to escape hungry predators. They use their legs to flick special hairs off their abdomen. These hairs stick in a predator's eyes. This gives the tarantula time to escape.

This tarantula will only attack when it feels threatened.

Snake attack

Snakes do not have arms or legs with which to catch animals. So how do they stop **prey** from escaping? Some snakes **inject** their prey with a poison called **venom**.

Venom and fangs

When a venomous snake spots an animal, it reaches forwards quickly and bites with long, hollow teeth called fangs. It injects its venom through the fangs into the prey. The venom works quickly. It **paralyzes** large prey to stop it moving, and kills smaller animals. Then the snake can swallow the prey whole, usually head first. If the prey is large, the snake can even loosen its jaw to fit it all in.

You can see the venom dripping from this snake's fangs. Snakes strike at high speed.

True story

CRUSHED TO DEATH

The python does not use venom to kill prey. It grabs an animal in its teeth, coils its body around the prey and squeezes. It squeezes so tightly that the prey animal cannot breathe. When the animal is dead, the snake loosens its jaw and swallows its prey whole.

Pythons rest in trees by coiling their bodies around branches.

Zebra journey

Every year, hundreds of thousands of zebras set out on an enormous journey across Africa. They **migrate** over huge distances. The zebras face dangerous **predators** and very deep rivers along the way. This way of travelling as a group is an **adaptation** that helps zebra herds to survive.

On the move

Zebras eat grasses and drink from pools of rainwater called watering holes. During the dry season in Africa, grass plants die. Zebra herds then travel to find more food and watering holes. Crossing rivers is especially dangerous, as crocodiles lie in wait to eat the weaker animals.

Zebras often travel with wildebeest and other migrating animals so they can warn each other about predators.

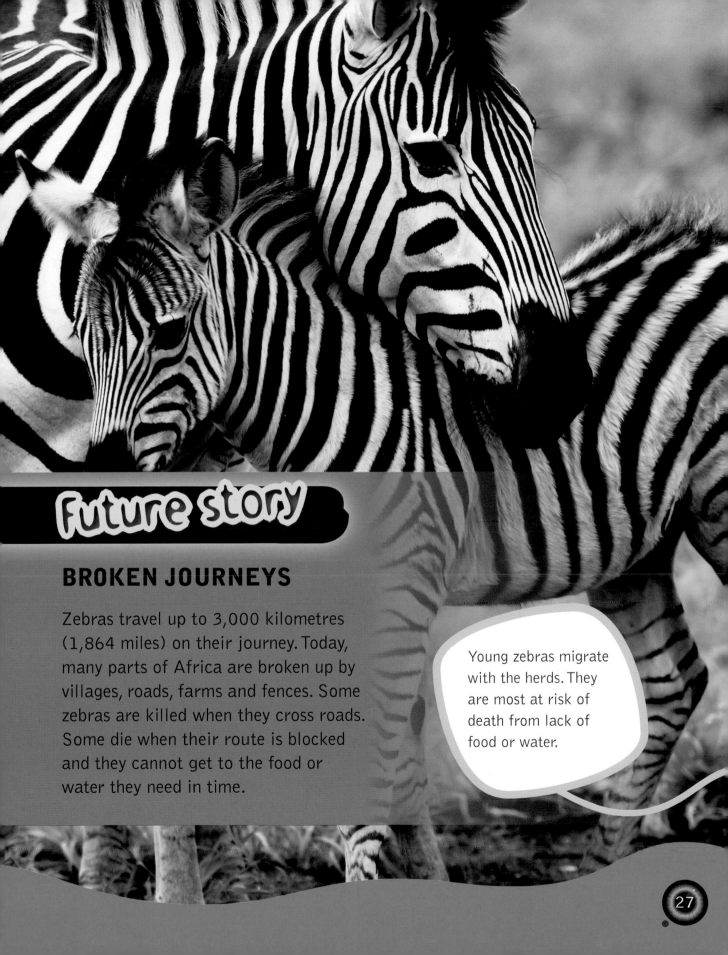

future story

BROKEN JOURNEYS

Zebras travel up to 3,000 kilometres (1,864 miles) on their journey. Today, many parts of Africa are broken up by villages, roads, farms and fences. Some zebras are killed when they cross roads. Some die when their route is blocked and they cannot get to the food or water they need in time.

Young zebras migrate with the herds. They are most at risk of death from lack of food or water.

Changing world

The world is constantly changing. People cut down trees and take over wild land for buildings, farms and factories. **Global warming** is melting ice. Rivers are drying up as the land warms. How will animals cope with these changes?

Changing quickly

Animals take thousands of years to adapt their bodies. However, some animals can adapt their behaviour much more quickly in order to survive. As wild areas are lost, animals such as raccoons, foxes and rats change their ways. Instead of living in the countryside, many have adapted to live in or near cities. There, they eat leftover food thrown away by people instead of wild food.

This raccoon is eating from a bird feeder. As people have taken over raccoon **habitats**, raccoons have adapted to live there, too. They even eat from rubbish bins.

True story

BAMBOO EATER

The giant panda is adapted to eat only bamboo. Its head is huge to hold the powerful jaw muscles it needs to chew this tough plant. However, because it eats only one type of food, the panda is in danger. Bamboo forests have been cut down and roads and villages now block many panda paths to other forests.

Although giant pandas are **endangered** animals, the Chinese government is creating panda **reserves** where they can live safely.

Glossary

abdomen part of the body that contains the stomach and gut

adaptation slow process of change that helps animals and plants to survive in their environments

bask lie in sunlight to soak up its warmth

blubber thick layer of fat beneath an animal's skin. Blubber helps an animal to keep warm.

camouflage body patterns or colours that help animals blend in with their surroundings

compete try to be the best, or to try to beat another

endangered in danger of dying out

global warming rise in Earth's temperature

habitat place in which an animal lives

inflated filled with air

inject make a hole in the surface of an animal's skin and to then push a liquid into its body

marking pattern on an animal's body

mate animal of the opposite sex to reproduce and have young with

migrate when an animal travels from place to place in order to find food or to have babies

paralyze stop something moving

predator animal that hunts and eats another animal

prey animal that is eaten by other animals

reserve place in which animals can live safely

stalk hide from an animal while hunting it

venom poisonous liquid that an animal uses to kill another animal

Find out more

Books

Adapted to Survive series, Angela Royston (Raintree, 2014)

Amazing Animal Survivors (Read Me! Animal Superpowers), John Townsend (Raintree, 2012)

Stinky Skunks and Other Animal Adaptations (Disgusting and Dreadful Science), Anna Claybourne (Franklin Watts, 2014)

Websites

www.bbc.co.uk/nature/adaptations
Find out more about all sorts of animal and plant adaptations.

www.ecokids.ca/pub/eco_info/topics/climate/adaptations
Try this fun quiz to match each animal with its adaptation.

www.nhm.ac.uk/kids-only/life
Visit the Natural History Museum's website to find out how animals have adapted to just about every place on Earth.

Index

blubber 20
body shape 6, 9, 12, 14, 16, 29

camouflage 7, 11, 17, 18
chameleons 18–19
cheetahs 16–17
crocodiles 14–15, 26

feeding 4, 6, 8, 9, 10, 12, 14,
   21, 22, 23, 24, 25, 26, 27,
   28, 29
foxes 28
frigate birds 5

giant pandas 29
giraffes 8–9
global warming 21, 28
great white sharks 6–7

hunting 4, 6, 10, 13, 16, 17

mate 4, 5, 18
migration 26–27
moles 4

owls 10–11

polar bears 20–21
predators 10, 12, 15, 19, 21,
   22, 23, 26
prey 6, 7, 10, 11, 14, 16, 17,
   18, 19, 21, 22, 24, 25
pythons 25

raccoons 28
rats 28
reserves 29

sight 4, 10, 11, 17, 19
smell 4, 6
snakes 23, 24, 25
spider monkeys 12–13
spiders 22–23

tarantulas 23
teeth 4, 6, 14, 15, 24, 25

zebras 26–27